Presented to

_____

From

_____

Date

_____

To Larry & Martha Holmes

Thank you, Mom & Dad, for loving me,
helping me, feeding me, clothing me,
and training me up to love God's Word.
Because of your faithfulness, I am better able
to do the same with our three kids.

Copyright © 2013 by Christian Art Kids, an imprint of Christian Art Publishers,
PO Box 1599, Vereeniging, 1930, RSA

359 Longview Drive, Bloomingdale, IL, 60108, USA

First edition 2013

Cover designed by Christian Art Kids

Text Copyright © 2009 by Andy Holmes

Art Copyright © 2009 by Tim O'Connor
All rights reserved.

Scripture quotations are taken from the *Holy Bible*, English Standard Version.
Copyright © 2001 by Crossway Bibles, a division of Good News Publishers.
Used by permission. All rights reserved.

Set in Aviner LT Std 65 Medium on 14 pt by Christian Art Kids

Printed in China

ISBN 978-1-4321-0561-7

Contents

THE NEW TESTAMENT

Introduction

Hi fellow parent!

Whenever I study God's Word, I am always amazed at God's faithfulness. We see it in the first story of Adam and Eve. God lovingly creates a thoroughly satisfying world for His children and still they revolt. God provides them with not only the bare essentials for living but much more than they could ever need. Still, they want more.

More options. More power. More excitement. Maybe that's how it felt to them, but summed up, they wanted the very thing that derails us each day: control. They wanted to be in charge, to determine their own steps, find their own way, blaze their own trail, forge their own design. Even if it killed them – which it ultimately did.

Truth is, had it been me in that garden of delights, I would have sampled that same fruit. And you would have, too. We prove that daily. That's why I love seeing God's faithfulness! God simply does not give up on us! Lamentations 3:22-24 says it beautifully: "The steadfast love of the Lord NEVER ceases; His mercies NEVER come to an end. They are NEW EVERY MORNING! GREAT is His faithfulness!"

As we study God's Word, we discover this transformational reality over and over. As that truth permeates our souls, it softens our hardened hearts and we come to rest on our Creator's lap. God's kindness can then lead us to repentance. When we embrace God's kind faithfulness, we are changed. Little by little, from glory to glory!

God wants this for our children, too. Training our children to not only love God's Word but to actually *know* God's Word is the best thing we can do for them as parents.

This concerns their salvation. This is God's command to us and not simply His casual suggestion or wishful hope.

This can feel like a daunting task. How do we do it? Where do we start when we cannot even pronounce Habakkuk?

The Big Story Bible was written to help you begin that journey with your child. It is a prayerful, careful attempt to entice your child into parts of God's Word and, in doing so, to captivate their interest in God's Word.

I call it *The Big Story Bible* because I hope to present the stories in a more connected or panoramic way. I want to help your child to see the "big picture" of God revealing Himself through individuals, families and nations; and how this reaches its crescendo in Christ. In fact, I focus the entirety of the New Testament stories exclusively on Christ.

Christ is the Big Picture.

Blessings!

Andy Holmes
andy@andyholmes.com
www.andyholmes.com

The Old Testament

The Beginning
Genesis 1

God is bigger than big.
Larger than large.
Huger than huge.
How big exactly?
Words cannot tell us.
And, if they could,
   no brain could understand it.
Still, as humongous as God is,
nothing is so small that God does not know all about it.

Tiny ants? Those were God's idea.

"Watch how hard they work," God tells us. "You should work hard like that, too."

Teeny mustard seeds? God made those, too. "Watch how big they grow," God said.

"Great big wonderful things happen when you love Me."

The smallest whisper?
God hears everything.

God knows what you are going to say before
you even say it!
Big things, small things, God
made each one.
Then who made God?
Nobody. God has always been there.
What's God like? God is love.
God made the world in love.
God said, "Trees! Plants! Flowers!"
And just like that, they came to be.
Apple trees. Banana trees.
Coconut trees. Peach, pear, and
pecan trees, too!
God made great big trees.
God made little, bitty trees.
"Very good," God said.

"Sun! Moon! Stars!" God made these, too.

Stars may look little in the sky, but they are bigger than the earth itself!

Our sun is a star! It is huge, right? But most stars are even bigger and even farther away.

God filled the oceans with all kinds of creatures.

Too many to count! Big ones. Little ones. Gigantic ones. Tiny ones.

"Very good," God said again.

God made all kinds of animals to live on the land.
Big ones.
Little ones.
Fat ones.
Skinny ones.
Slithering ones.
Silly ones.

"And now," God said, the angels leaning over to see,
"Let's make a man to care for all that I have made."
Hello Adam.
Hello Eve.
God looked at everything He had made.
"Very good," God said. "Very good."

The First Family
Genesis 2:4-25

God sculpted a man out of dust from the ground. With as much delight as a child with clay, God sculpted. With the passion and skill of the greatest artist, God sculpted. "Ahh," God must have sighed with pleasure as He studied His masterpiece. "It is good," God said.

God breathed life into the new man's nose and the new man became *alive*.

"It is not good for man to be alone," God said.
"I will make for him a helper. A friend just right for him."

God made all the animals gather near the new man, Adam,
so Adam could make up names for each one of them.

"Cow. Dog. Salamander. Sparrow. Penguin. Duck. Goose. Owl."

It was a big job, Adam's first task.

Of course, no suitable helper was found among the animals for Adam. So God made Adam fall into a deep, deep sleep. While Adam slept, God took one of his ribs and built the rib into a brand-new creation: a woman.

"This is the bone of my bones, and the flesh of my flesh!" Adam said, no doubt overcome with joy. Instant friends. Instant family. The first of countless families to come.

Then God blessed them. "This is good," God said. "This is very good." It was a wonderful moment. "Have children," God told them. "Fill this big world with people. Take care of all that I have made here. Work the land. Keep watch over the animals. Be good and strong leaders."

God made all kinds of trees spring up from out of the ground. Then, smack-dab in the middle of the garden, God put two very special trees. Two one-of-a-kind trees!

One was called the Tree of Life and the other was called the Tree of the Knowledge of Good and Evil. "Do not eat from this tree," God instructed. "If you do, you'll die."

Adam and Eve

Genesis 2:15; 3

God placed Adam and Eve in a beautiful garden He had made. It had everything they would need: sunshine to keep them warm; stars to remind them God was always watching over them; water to refresh and clean; and more food than they could ever eat.

"Eat from any tree in the garden," God said, "except from the tree of good and bad. If you eat that fruit, you will surely die."

Sounded simple enough. Why would they even go near that tree when there were so many other delicious trees to eat from? No problem, right? Wrong. It was a *big* problem.

They met a talking serpent. "You will not die," he told them.
"But God said . . . " Eve began.
"Take a bite and see," the serpent hissed. "You will become as smart as God Himself."

This was, of course, the most dangerous lie of all of his lies. No one is as smart as God. But the thought of becoming so smart that they would no longer need God around to tell them what to do … well, it sort of took them over.

They bit.

He grinned.

God came.

They hid.

"You cannot stay in the garden," God explained. "Life will be much harder for you now."

God put mighty angels with flaming swords at the entrance of the garden to keep them out and away from the Tree of Life lest they eat of it and live forever in their broken condition.

Ah, but there is an even better garden awaiting us. For God loved the world so much that He gave His only Son so that anyone who believes in Him shall not perish but have eternal life.

Noah's Ark

Genesis 6-9

Many years had passed since Adam and Eve's disobedience in the garden. Adam and Eve had many children. Their children had children. Their children's children had children and – well, you get the idea.

Remember that lie the talking serpent told about being as smart as God? Well, that lie became a part of every person's thinking. Everyone – at one time or another – thought, *I can do whatever I want to do.* That kind of thinking leads people to do evil.

Soon, there was no one living to please God. People did only evil things. This broke God's heart. But Noah was a pleasure to the Lord. He always tried to obey God.

"Noah," God said. "I am going to destroy all mankind because people have become so evil, but I will keep you and your family safe. You are going to need a boat," God said.

Noah and his sons built the boat, following all of God's directions. It was gigantic!

Then God led every animal into the boat – a male and female of each.

"Go inside now, Noah," God said. "Take your family in, too. I am about to make it rain."

It rained hard night and day for forty days, lifting the large boat high above the flooded earth. Everything that lived on the land died.

As the waters drained, the boat settled on top of a mountain. Soon, other mountain peaks appeared. Finally, the earth was dry again.

"Come out now, Noah," God said. Noah and his family, and all of the animals came out. Noah built an altar and honored God with an offering to please God.

"Noah," God said, "I will never destroy the whole earth with a flood again." Then God sealed that promise with a rainbow. "This rainbow will always remind Me of my promise to you today."

The Tower of Babel

Genesis 11:1-9

After the flood, God called Noah and his sons out of the ark and gave them a new command: "Go," God said, "fill the earth."

Noah's son, Shem, had many children, grandchildren, great-grandchildren, and on it goes. Noah's son, Japheth, did the same. Noah's youngest son, Ham, did this, too. All the nations of the world began here. All of them spoke the same language.

At first, they obeyed God, but then the old lie the talking serpent told so many years ago caught hold of the people once again.

"We do not have to fill the earth," they said, their hearts growing hard. "We do not have to obey God," they declared. "We can do anything we want to!" they shouted. "*We are* in charge."

So they stopped walking, unpacked their things, tossed God's command aside and made a new plan of their very own.

"Come!" one called out, "Let us stay together – all of us! Let us build a city here! And let us build it *our* way."

"Let us build a tower, too!" others shouted, "Let us make it with bricks so it will last forever!"

They made stacks and stacks of hard-baked bricks.

They gathered sticky tar-like stuff to join the bricks together.

They stacked the bricks higher and higher until the tower seemed to reach the sky.

God saw the city and tower they were building. God knew this was only the beginning of the evil things they would do working together to please themselves.

This must be stopped, God decided.
So God did a miracle.
In an instant, He made them speak different languages. Suddenly, they could not understand one another!

One would ask for a brick and be handed a hammer.
One would ask for a saw and be given a brick.
Everyone was confused.
The work STOPPED,
and God scattered them all over the earth.

Abram and Lot

Genesis 12: 1-9, 13

"Abram," God said. "Leave your country and your people and your father's family, and go to the land I will lead you to."

When he was 75 years old, Abram and his wife, Sarai, and his nephew, Lot, packed up all their things, gathered all of their servants and left his homeland, his people, his father and his kin, and went to a land called Canaan.

"One day, I will give this land to your children," God told Abram. Abram built an altar there to honor God.
They traveled on.

Abram became very rich. He had lots of cows and goats and sheep. Abram also had a lot of silver and gold. Abram's nephew, Lot, also became rich in cattle and possessions. They had so many servants, animals and possessions that things became crowded.

"Hey, watch where you are going!" one of Abram's servants would shout to one of Lot's servants.

"You watch where you are going!" Lot's servant would shout back.

Soon there were so many arguments something had to be done about it.

"It is too crowded," Abram told Lot. "We each need our own space." Abram pointed to the land that surrounded them. "You pick, Lot," Abram said. "If you choose to go to the left, I will take the land to the right. Or, if you pick the land to the right, I will take the land to the left. You get first choice."

Lot decided to live in the lush, green plains near the Jordan river. Abram went back to Canaan.

Abram and the Starry, Starry Night

Genesis 17:15-19; 18:1-15; 21:1-6

Abram had lots of silver and lots of gold.

Abram had lots of sheep and lots of cattle.

There is one thing Abram did not have: children. Abram and Sarai had no children at all, though they had longed for a child for many years.

"O Lord," Abram cried, "You have given me so much, but I have no child to share these gifts with."

God said, "I will give you a son, Abram." God led Abram outside. "Look up, Abram." Abram stared at the star-filled sky. "Count them," God said, knowing there were far too many. "No one will be able to count your children either."

Many years passed. God appeared again to Abram who was now nearly 100 years old. "Abram," God said. "You will now be called 'Abraham' and Sarai will be 'Sarah'. I will make you the father of many nations and kings." Abraham fell facedown, laughed and thought, *Will my Sarah become a mother at 90 years of age?* God heard Abraham's thoughts and answered, "Yes, Sarah will, and you will name the baby 'Isaac'."

Later, God visited Abraham once again. Abraham looked up and saw three men. He ran to meet them and bowed. He washed their feet and fed them under a shady tree. "Where is Sarah?" they asked. Sarah stood at the door of their tent, straining to hear.

Then the Lord said, "When I come back next year, Sarah will have a baby boy." Sarah laughed and thought, *Now that I am old and worn out, I will have a baby?* Then God said, "Abraham, why did Sarah laugh? Is anything too hard for the Lord?"

The Lord was kind to Sarah and she had a baby the very next year. They named him 'Isaac'.

A Wife for Isaac

Genesis 24

Isaac grew and soon he was a young man. Abraham, however, was a very old man. He called his chief servant. "I am sending you to my home country to find a wife for Isaac." The servant promised he would do as Abraham asked.

"What if the girl is not willing to come back with me?" the servant said. "Shall I then take Isaac there?"

"No!" Abraham said firmly. "God will send His angel with you to bless this journey to find a wife for Isaac. If she is unwilling to come back here with you then you are free from your promise."

The servant took ten camels and loaded them up with gifts. When he arrived at Nahor, he made his camels kneel near the well just outside the town. "O Lord, God of my master Abraham," he prayed, "show kindness to Abraham. Lead me to the girl You have chosen for Isaac. As a sign to me, let her offer to give my camels water to drink."

Before he had even finished his prayer, he saw a beautiful girl named Rebekah filling her jar with water. "Please, give me a drink," he said. "Drink, my lord," she answered. "I will give water to your camels, too," she said. And she did.

The servant bowed and prayed, "Praise be to the Lord, the God of my master Abraham!"

The servant told Rebekah's family about Abraham and Isaac. He told them how God led him straight to Rebekah. Rebekah's father and brother said, "This is God's will."

The servant gave them the gifts he had packed.
"Will you go with this man, Rebekah?" they
asked. Rebekah smiled. "I will go," she said.
Isaac loved Rebekah and she became
his wife.

Jacob and Esau
Genesis 27:1-38

If you have a brother or sister, chances are, you have gotten into a squabble or two, but Jacob and Esau started wrestling before they were even born! Esau was born first, but just barely – Jacob's tiny hand was clenched around Esau's heel!

Once, Esau came home starving. He had been hunting wild animals. "Hurry, Jacob!" he gasped. "Give me some stew!" Jacob had a sneaky idea. "First you give me something I want," he said. "Give me your firstborn birthrights." "I am about to die here!" Esau snapped back. "Take the birthrights! Just give me some stew!"

When Isaac, their father, was old and nearly blind, he told Esau to go hunting. "Bring back something tasty for me to eat. It is time for me to give you my special blessing."

As soon as Esau left, Rebekah (Jacob's mother) told Jacob, "Your father is going to give Esau his special blessing." Rebekah leaned closer and whispered, "I want you to get the blessing instead. So, you are going to trick your father."

"But Esau's hairy and I am not, Mother." "I have got an idea for that," she said. "Now, go get two young goats from the flock so I can make one of your father's favorite meals."

Rebekah put goat's hair on Jacob's arm, neck and hand, and gave him Esau's best clothes to wear. "Take this meal to your father," she said.

"Who's there?" Isaac asked. "It is me, Esau, your firstborn," Jacob answered. "I have done what you asked. Please eat so you can bless me." Isaac squinted. "Come closer," he said, "so I can touch you and know for sure." Isaac rubbed Jacob's arms and hands. "The voice is Jacob's, but the hands are Esau's." Then Isaac blessed him.

Jacob left quickly and Esau entered just after him. "My father," he said, "sit up and eat so you can bless me." Isaac was confused. "Who are you?" "I am your firstborn son, Esau." Isaac shook with rage. "Your brother Jacob has taken your blessing from you." Esau cried bitterly.

Joseph and His Brothers

Genesis 37

When Jacob was a man,
God blessed him and said,
"From now on, Jacob,
your name will be Israel."
Jacob, now called Israel, had
lots of sons. Of all his sons, he
loved Joseph the most. Because
of this, Israel's other sons hated
Joseph. They could not even speak a
single kind word to him.

God gave Joseph secret messages through his dreams – messages which would one day come true. His dreams made his brothers hate him even more – especially the one where all of them bowed down to him. "I dreamt we were gathering grain into bundles," Joseph told his brothers. "Suddenly, my bundle stood up straight while all of your bundles bowed down to it." His brothers were mad to their toes. "Do you really think you are going to rule over us?" they said, and they hated him even more.

One day, Joseph brought food to his brothers. When they saw him wearing the special coat Israel gave him, they decided right then and there to kill him. "Here comes dreamer boy!" one said with a smirk, and they all laughed.

They tore the coat off Joseph then threw him in a dry well. "Let's see what will come of all those dumb dreams now!" one sneered.

Just then, travelers passed by. "Let's sell him instead," said Judah. They sold Joseph and smeared goat's blood on his coat.

"Look, Father," the brothers said, pretending to be upset. "Is this Joseph's coat?" Jacob's heart broke. "Joseph! Joseph!" he cried. "Surely a wild animal killed him." All of his sons and daughters tried to comfort him. "Leave me alone," he told them. "I will cry over this till the day I die."

Joseph In Egypt

Genesis 39-41

Joseph begged his brothers to save him, but they would not listen. The travelers took him to Egypt and sold him to Potiphar. Potiphar liked Joseph and soon put him in charge of everything. Then, Potiphar's wife lied about Joseph so Potiphar put Joseph in prison.

Even in jail, God took care of Joseph. Soon, the prison boss put Joseph in charge. Two men who used to work for Pharaoh were thrown into prison. Each dreamt a disturbing dream. "We had dreams that confuse us," they said.

"Tell me your dreams," Joseph said.

"God knows what they mean."

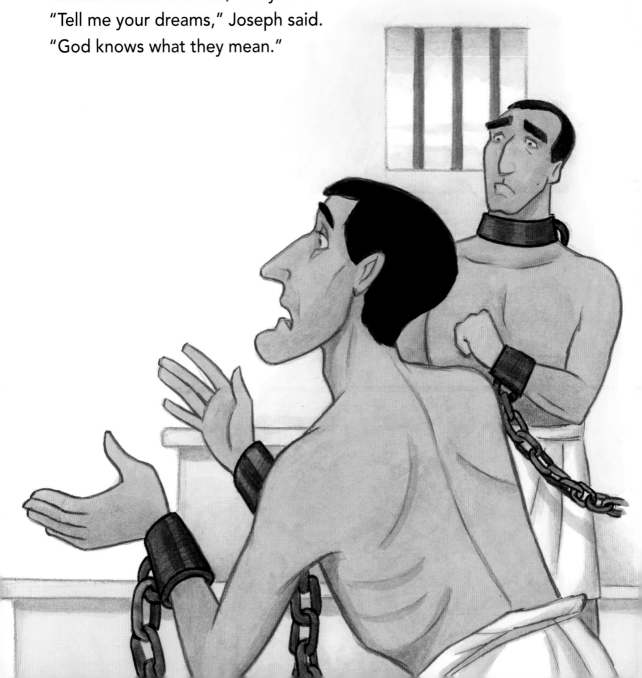

Joseph explained their dreams. Pharaoh's cupbearer's dream had a happy ending. Pharaoh's baker's dream did not. "Tell Pharaoh about me when you get your old job back," Joseph said. "Will do!" the cupbearer promised, but once he was back in Pharaoh's palace, the cupbearer forgot all about Joseph and how he had helped him.

Two long years later, Pharaoh himself had a dream. It disturbed him greatly. No one could tell him what it meant. That's when the cupbearer remembered Joseph.

"I know a man who can help!" he told Pharaoh. "Bring Joseph to me at once!" Pharaoh commanded.

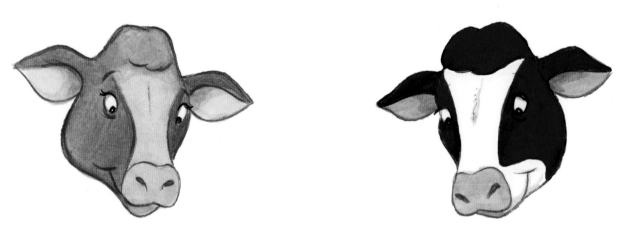

"In my dream there were seven fat cows, then seven skinny cows," Pharaoh told Joseph. "Then the skinny cows ate the fat cows. Can you explain this dream to me?"

"God can," Joseph answered. "The seven fat cows mean seven good years of crops. The seven skinny cows mean seven

bad years. You must save up food during the seven good years or else everyone will starve during the seven bad years."

Pharaoh was amazed. "You will be in charge of this, Joseph," he said. "After me, no one will be as powerful as you."

Joseph Forgives His Brothers

Genesis 42:1-24; 45:3-7

Joseph collected food during the seven good years and stored it in huge barns in each city. He stored up so much grain they could not measure it. Then, just as Pharaoh's dream had warned, the seven good years came to a sudden end.

The seven bad years dried up all the fields. Nothing grew. In time, the people ran out of food and ran to Pharaoh. "Help us!" they wailed. "Do not let us starve to death!" "Go to Joseph," Pharaoh told them, and Joseph took care of them with the food he had stored up.

People from other countries also came to Joseph to buy grain. Jacob (Joseph's father who is also called 'Israel') told his sons, "Go to Egypt. Buy food there or we will starve."

When his brothers arrived, they bowed to Joseph – just like his dream had shown. Joseph recognized them, but they did not recognize him. "We have come to buy food," they said. "No!" Joseph answered. "You are spies!" And he put them in jail for three days. "Bring me your youngest brother and I will believe you," Joseph said.

"We are being punished for what we did," they argued with each other. "Joseph screamed for us to help him, but we would not listen." Joseph turned away to cry secretly. They didn't know he could understand them.

When they came back with Benjamin (the youngest brother), Joseph raced out of the room to hide his tears. He washed his face, then returned. Soon, he couldn't hold back his feelings any longer. "I am Joseph!" he told them. At first, his brothers were terrified, but Joseph hugged and kissed them and said, "God sent me here, not you." And they all cried and hugged some more.

Baby Moses

Exodus 1-2

Many years after Jacob, also called 'Israel', and his family died, Egypt had a new king. He was afraid of the Israelites. "There are too many of them," he said. "We must make them our slaves before they turn on us."

"You there!" an Egyptian slave master snapped, "Make more bricks!"
"Faster!" another Egyptian slave master yelled, "Gather more wheat!"
"Hurry!" still another Egyptian master screamed. "Build faster!"

Even worse, the king told the midwives to kill the Israelites' baby boys. The midwives feared God so they did not obey the king's evil orders.

Then the king gave the most evil order of all: "Throw all the Israelite boys into the river to die!"

Now Amram and Jochebed had a baby boy. Jochebed hid him for three months. When she could not hide him any longer, she put him in a basket and hid the basket among the reeds near the bank of the river. Miriam, the baby's sister, watched.

The king's daughter saw the basket, and discovered the baby. He was crying and his tiny tears made her feel sad for him. Brave Miriam wasted no time. She ran to the princess "Shall I find an Israelite woman to care for the baby for you?" she asked. "Yes," the princess answered.

Miriam brought her mother. "Care for this baby for me," the princess told Jochebed. "I will pay you." When the baby was older, Jochebed took her son back to the princess. "I will name you 'Moses'," the princess said. "I will be your mother and you will be my son." So Moses grew up in the palace of the king.

Moses and the Burning Bush
Exodus 3; 4:1-17

Pharaoh's daughter raised Moses in the palace as her own son. On the outside, Moses looked like Egyptian royalty, but on the inside, Moses knew otherwise. Moses was a Hebrew – like the slaves Pharaoh so cruelly mistreated.

One day, as he watched an Egyptian beating a Hebrew – one of his own people – his anger burned so hot, he killed the Egyptian. When Pharaoh found out, he tried to kill Moses. Fearing for his life, Moses ran away to a town called Midian.

In time, Moses married and became a father and a shepherd. Many years passed.

One day, while Moses was tending sheep in the desert, he noticed a bush was on fire. Strangely, the bush did not burn up even though the fire raged. *That's odd*, Moses thought. Stepping closer Moses heard God calling his name. "Stop!" God told him. "Take off your sandals. You are standing on holy ground." Moses obeyed.

"I am the God of your father, the God of Abraham, the God of Isaac and the God of Jacob," God said. Moses hid his face, afraid to look at God. "I am sending you to Pharaoh. You are going to lead My suffering people out of Egypt."

"Me?" Moses said.

"I will be with you, Moses," God said.

"What if they don't believe me?" Moses said. "Who should I say sent me?"

"Tell the Hebrews: 'I AM has sent me to you.'" God said.

"But what if they still do not believe me?" Moses said.

"Throw your staff onto the ground," God said, and when Moses did, his staff became a snake.

Moses jumped back. "Now, pick it up," God said, and when Moses did, the snake turned back into a staff. "Now, put your hand inside your cloak, Moses." Moses obeyed. When he pulled his hand out of his cloak, it was covered with snowy-white sores. Moses was startled. "Put it back in," God said, and when Moses did, his hand was healthy again.

"But, Lord," Moses said, "I am a poor speaker."

God asked, "Did I not give you a mouth? Go, I will teach you what to say."

Finally, Moses begged, "Please, God, send someone else!"

The Lord's anger was stirred. "Your brother, Aaron, may go with you. He will do the talking and you will perform the miraculous signs. Now, go!"

"Let My People Go"

Exodus 7-10

Obeying God does not always make life easier. Many times, it makes it harder. Oh, but there's power, power, wonder-working power when we do what God commands – as Moses found out.

The Hebrews bowed down and worshiped God when they learned from Moses and Aaron that the Lord saw their misery and cared about them. Pharaoh did the opposite.

"Pharaoh," Moses and Aaron said, "The Lord, the God of the Hebrews, says: 'Let My people go'."

Pharaoh answered, "Who is the Lord that I should obey Him? I do not know Him and I will not let them go." Indeed, Pharaoh made the Hebrew slaves work even harder.

"Lord," Moses cried, "is this why You sent me – to bring Your people trouble?"

The Lord answered, "Now you will see My mighty hand and Pharaoh will let My people go."

"Pharaoh," Moses said, "If you do not let the Hebrews go, God will plague your country with frogs. They will fill your palace, your bedroom – even your bed." Pharaoh said, "I will not let them go."

Soon frogs were everywhere. Pharaoh called Moses to him. "Pray to the Lord to take these frogs away and I will let the Hebrews go." Moses prayed and God answered, but when the frogs were gone, Pharaoh changed his mind. "No!" he said. "The Hebrews stay!"

So God sent other plagues: gnats, flies, death of the Egyptians' animals, painful sores, hailstorms, locusts and three days of total darkness. Still, Pharaoh said, "NO!"

The final plague would be the worst of all.

Passover: The Final Plague

Exodus 11-12

Moses and Aaron told Pharaoh all God commanded. Still, Pharaoh said, "No". It seemed no matter how bad things got, Pharaoh would not change his mind. So, God sent Moses to Pharaoh one last time.

"The Lord says every firstborn son in Egypt will die tonight," Moses told Pharaoh, "Even your son. It will be the saddest day ever in Egypt. But the Hebrew children," Moses added, "will be kept safe. Then you will let God's people go."

God sent Moses to the Hebrews. "Each family must take a perfect, young lamb, and offer it to the Lord." Moses explained. "God wants you to put some of the blood around your doorframes. Cook the meat over the fire, along with bitter herbs and flat bread. You are to eat this meal in a hurry, dressed and packed and ready to leave. This is God's Passover meal." Moses said.

"The blood protects you. When God sees the blood, all the children in that house will be safe because God will pass over that house. This is a day you will remember and celebrate."

The Hebrews obeyed. God passed over Egypt. He struck down the Egyptians' homes, but spared the Hebrews. All of Egypt cried bitterly. "Go!" Pharaoh told Moses and Aaron. "Leave!"

The Hebrews left that very night, quickly gathering as many of their things as they could carry – along with gifts of silver and gold and clothing from the Egyptians. "Go!" the Egyptians hurried them, "or we will all die!"

Crossing the Red Sea

Exodus 13:17-22; 14

God led them by day with a pillar of cloud and by night with a pillar of fire to light their way.

When Pharaoh learned they were gone, he changed his mind. "What have I done?" he said. "Who will do all their work?" Pharaoh got in his chariot, rallied his army and chased after them.

When the Israelites saw them, they were scared and cried out to Moses. "Why have you brought us out here to die in the desert?"

"Do not be afraid," Moses told them. "God will take care of us!"

"Raise your staff, Moses," God told him. "Stretch out your hand over the sea."

Moses obeyed and God pushed the sea back with a strong wind. The water was split in two and the Israelites walked through on dry ground, with a wall of water on their right side and on their left side.

Pharaoh and his army followed them into the open sea and the Lord told Moses to stretch his hand over the sea again. Moses did and God made the walls of water come back together. Pharaoh's army was drowned.

The Israelites saw God's awesome power and put their trust in Him and in Moses.

The Golden Calf

Exodus 32

God had certainly rescued His people in an amazing way. Can you imagine walking on dry ground between those walls of water? That's not the kind of thing you could easily forget and yet, God's children seemed to do exactly that. They forgot that the Lord would always take care of them. Instead of trusting God, they grumbled.

When they could not find water to drink, they grumbled. Again, God did an amazing thing. "Moses," God said, "Throw this piece of wood into the bitter water." Moses did and the water turned sweet.

When they could not find food, they grumbled. "If only God would have left us in Egypt!" they wailed. "We had tons of food there!" So God sent quail meat and a secret kind of food they called 'manna'. They called it 'manna' because 'manna' means "What is it?" They had never seen it before. It was white and tasted like honey wafers. "God will send us manna each day," Moses told them. "Trust God and do not keep it until morning." But some disobeyed and, by morning, it was stinky and full of maggots.

When Moses went up on the mountain to meet with God, the people forgot about God altogether. "Moses has left us!" they cried. "Let us make up our own god!" So they melted their earrings and sculpted a golden calf and called it their 'god'. Craziness followed.

Then God told Moses, "Go down, your people have turned against Me." Moses went and found them dancing to their golden idol. He was so mad he took the calf, ground it into powder, scattered it on the water and forced them to drink it. "This is a horrible sin you have done!"

The Battle of Jericho
Joshua 5:13-15; 6:1-24

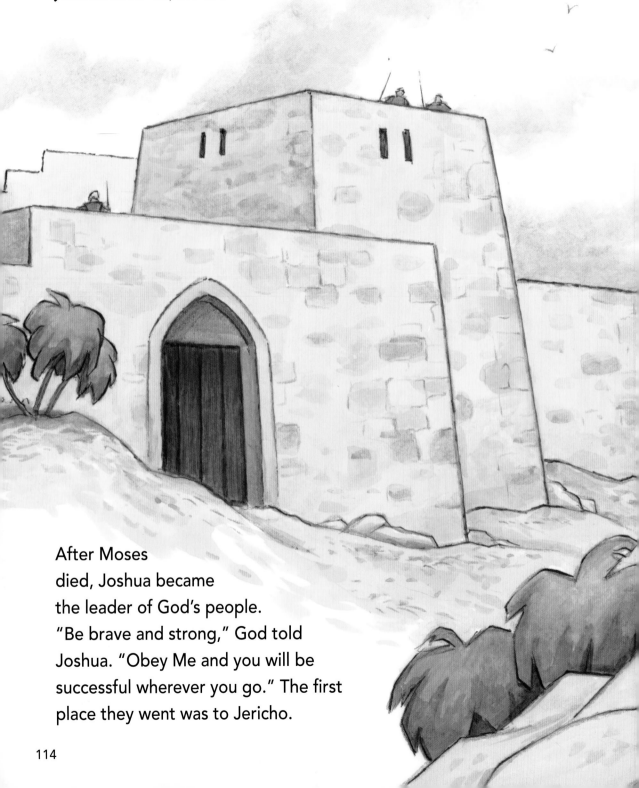

After Moses
died, Joshua became
the leader of God's people.
"Be brave and strong," God told
Joshua. "Obey Me and you will be
successful wherever you go." The first
place they went was to Jericho.

114

Jericho was a city surrounded by a thick, stone wall. How thick? As thick as a man is tall! And, if that wasn't enough to discourage anyone from trying to break into the city, some say there was yet another wall – twice as thick – inside that wall! Yes, the folks who lived in Jericho had good reason to sleep peacefully each night, knowing how safely their city was protected from anyone who wanted to attack them.

Then again, those people did not know how amazingly powerful God is, but Joshua knew.

One day Joshua saw a man standing in front of him. He was holding a sword. Joshua walked right up to him and asked plainly, "Are you for us or are you for our enemies?" "Neither," the soldier told him, "but as commander of the army of the Lord I have now come." As soon as he heard these words, Joshua fell to the ground. "What message does my Lord have for His servant?"

"Take off your sandals," the commander told him, "you are standing on holy ground." Joshua obeyed.

The Lord told Joshua that He was giving them the city of Jericho in a most unusual way. "March with all your soldiers around the city once each day for six days," God told him. "Have seven priests carry trumpets of rams' horns in front of the ark of the covenant." (The ark of the covenant was a specially made box where they kept the stone tablets

with the Ten Commandments, Aaron's rod and manna.)

Joshua listened well and told the people what God had told him: "Then, on the seventh day," Joshua said, "God said for us to march around the city seven times with the priests blowing the trumpets. Then when the priests sound a loud blast, all of us will shout as loud as we can and the walls of Jericho will fall down and we can go into the city to fight."

And that's just what they did. They marched around the city once on the first day, then they returned to their camp for the night. Then they marched around the city once on the second and then returned to their camp. They did this for six days. Then, just as the Lord commanded them to do, they marched around the city seven times on the seventh day and when the priests blew a long blast on their trumpets, all of them shouted with all their might and those strong, thick walls came tumbling down.

119

Gideon's Battle
Judges 6-7

Would you use a pickle to paint a house or spaghetti to tie your shoes? They might work for a little while – *maybe* – but you would probably need a pretty good reason before you'd ever even think of trying it.

Well, Gideon tried something almost as silly. Instead of threshing wheat on a threshing floor on a hilltop where the wind would blow the dust away from your face and eyes while you worked, Gideon threshed the wheat in the tub-like bottom of a winepress. What a dusty mess!

Why did Gideon do this? The same reason he and many of his Israelite neighbors ran away to live in caves: to hide from the mean Midianites who were making life absolutely miserable for them.

Talk about bullies! Whenever an Israelite tried to grow some food, the Midianites would ruin it. If an Israelite had a donkey or cow or a lamb, the Midianites would steal it or kill it. And there were so many Midianites, the smartest grown-up in the world could not count them all.

One day while Gideon was threshing wheat in a winepress – no doubt coughing his head off – an angel of the Lord appeared to him and said, "The Lord is with you, mighty warrior." Gideon probably looked more like the loser in a mud fight than a mighty warrior – but not to God.

"I am sending you to save Israel from the Midianites," God told him. Gideon gulped. "But, Lord," he said, "I come from the weakest of Israelites and I am the baby in my family."

"I will be with you," the Lord promised.

Gideon gathered up an army of men, but God told him, "There are too many men. This is My battle to win, not yours. Send the men who are frightened home." Gideon obeyed and twenty-two thousand frightened men went home and ten thousand men stayed on.

"Still too many," God said and then he whittled Gideon's army down to only three-hundred men.

Late one night, God told Gideon to sneak into the Midianite camp. "Listen to what the Midianite soldiers are saying," God told him, "and you will not be afraid to attack them."

Gideon and Purah tiptoed down near the Midianites' camp. Although there were still too many Midianite soldiers to count, here's what Gideon heard them saying: "I had a dream," one Midianite told his friend, "that a round loaf of bread tumbled into camp and crushed our tents." The other Midianite's eyes widened with fear. "This dream means that the sword of Gideon will destroy us! God will make sure that this happens!"

Gideon was thrilled, "God be praised!" Gideon returned to his
camp and told his soldiers about it. He divided the men into three
groups and gave everyone a trumpet and a jar with a torch inside it.
"Follow me," he told them, "and do what I do."

They tiptoed back to the Midianites' camp and hid all around it. Then – as quick as a flash – Gideon and the men in his group blew their trumpets and broke their jars and shouted: "A sword for the Lord and for Gideon!" Immediately, the other two groups did the same.

The Midianite army woke up in a fright and began fighting each other in the dark. Those who did not die right there, ran away in the night only to be chased down by Gideon's men.

Samson: The Strongest Man Alive

Judges 16

Once again God's people turned away from Him. Once again they found themselves being ruled over by powerful and cruel people – the Philistines. Once again, God saw their pain and sent someone to help them. His name was Samson, and God made him stronger than a lion.

Samson did not allow the Philistines to bully him like they bullied the rest of the Israelites:

- When the Philistines cheated to win a riddle contest with Samson, he beat up thirty of their men and took their clothes to pay the prize.
- When the Philistines cheated Samson out of marrying his bride-to-be, he caught three hundred foxes, tied them tail to tail in pairs, fastened torches to their tails, lit them and let them loose. The foxes ran through the Philistines' grain fields and vineyards and olive groves with the torches on fire behind them.
- When they gathered an army of three thousand men to attack Samson, the Spirit of the Lord filled Samson with enough power to kill one thousand of them and to send the others running off scared.

No matter what they tried, Samson was too powerful for them. "We have to find the secret of his amazing power," they decided. And that's when they met Delilah – Samson's girlfriend.

"Tell me the secret of your great strength," Delilah whispered, "and how you can be made weak enough to capture." Samson, who loved to play jokes and pranks, said, "If someone ties me with seven fresh strings that have never been dried, I will become as weak as any other man."

Delilah told the Philistines what Samson had said and they gave her seven strings and sent a group of men to capture him, but when she tied him and the men tried to grab him, Samson broke the strings as if they were paper and the men could not overpower him.

"You lied to me, Samson," Delilah pouted. "Tell me the true secret of your power." Once again Samson played a prank on her. "If you tie me with ropes that have never been used, I will be as weak as any other man."

Again, Delilah believed him and, again, she was disappointed. "How can you say you love me and yet keep this secret from me?" Delilah cried and nagged him day after day until Samson finally told her the truth: "If you shave my head, I will become as weak as any other man."

Once again, Delilah told the Philistines what Samson had said and, once Samson had fallen asleep, they cut off his hair and Samson was too weak to protect himself. The Philistines blinded Samson, put shackles on him and threw him in prison. "Our god has delivered Samson to us," they bragged.

But while he was in prison, Samson's hair began to grow back.

One day, during a wild celebration in their temple, some Philistines shouted, "Bring Samson out so we can laugh at him!" They brought Samson out, stood him between the two stone pillars that held up the temple and made a fool of him. Samson told the young man who was guarding him to help him touch the pillars so he could rest.

"Master God," Samson cried out. "Please give me Your power just once more and let me pay these Philistines back. And let me die with them." And God did. Samson pushed the pillars apart which brought the whole temple down and killed all the Philistine rulers and people in it – Samson, too.

Ruth and Naomi

Ruth 1-4

Times were tough for Naomi. Her husband had died. Her grown sons had died. And, if things were not bad enough, there wasn't enough food in the land for everyone to eat. Naomi heard there was food in Moab so she decided to go there.

"I am too old to have more sons for you to marry," Naomi told her daughter-in-laws, Orpah and Ruth. "Go back to your mothers' homes and find husbands – why would you come with me?"

They all cried and hugged and cried some more. "Go home," Naomi urged them. Finally, Orpah agreed to leave, but no matter what Naomi said, Ruth wouldn't budge. "I am going where you go and staying where you stay. Your people will be my people and your God my God." When Naomi saw how set on staying Ruth was, she didn't say any more about it.

Naomi and Ruth went to Bethlehem. It was time to gather the barley from the nearby fields so Ruth said, "Let me go pick the leftover grain so we'll have something to eat." Naomi agreed it was a good idea. As it turned out, Ruth found leftovers in a field belonging to a man named Boaz.

"The Lord be with you," Boaz told the workers as he arrived. "The Lord bless you!" they called back. When Boaz saw Ruth, he asked his foreman about her. "She's the one who came with Naomi. She's been working hard since this morning."

"You may stay here with my servant girls," Boaz told Ruth. "You will be safe. May God repay you for the kindness you are showing to Naomi." After that, Boaz told his workers to make sure she found plenty of grain to take home.

Boaz was actually Naomi's relative. In time, Boaz married Ruth and took care of Naomi, too. "Praise be to God!" the women sang out. "God has given Naomi a brand-new family!"

God Speaks to Samuel

1 Samuel 1; 3

Sweet Hannah wanted a baby more than anything else in the world. Once, after dinner, Hannah went to the temple to pray about it. "Mighty God," she cried, "if You will give me a son," she sobbed, "I will give him to You, God, for all the days of his life." Hannah cried so hard as she prayed, you could hardly understand the words she was saying. Eli, the priest who was sitting by the doorpost of the temple, overheard her mumblings and thought she was drunk.

"Stop getting drunk," Eli told her, but Hannah explained: "I am not drunk. I haven't drank beer or wine. I am just very, very sad and I was pouring my heart out to God." Eli, no doubt relieved, said, "Go in peace, and may the Lord give you what you have asked for." And God did.

Hannah named the baby boy 'Samuel' and as soon as the boy was old enough to walk, she took him to the temple. "I am the woman who prayed here beside you. I asked God for a son and He gave me one. So, now, as I promised, I give him to the Lord."

Samuel grew up in the temple, serving the Lord under Eli the priest. Each year, Hannah made a little robe for Samuel and gave it to him when she went up to the temple to worship God.

One night while Samuel was sleeping, he heard his name being called: "Samuel, Samuel." The boy got up, ran to Eli and said, "I am here – you called me." But Eli told him, "I did not call you. Go back to bed." So Samuel went back to sleep.

Then he heard it again: "Samuel, Samuel."

Once again, Samuel went to Eli. "Yes? I am here."

"My boy," Eli told him, "I did not call you. Go back to bed."

Again, he heard someone calling him: "Samuel, Samuel." Again, he went to Eli. "Here I am." That's when Eli realized it was God who was calling him. "Samuel," Eli explained, "Go back to bed and if you hear a voice again, say, 'Speak, Lord, Your servant is listening.'" And God spoke to Samuel.

Samuel grew up and God was with him and all the things God spoke through Samuel came true.

A Shepherd Boy Becomes King

1 Samuel 8-10, 16

When Samuel grew old, he put his sons in charge of Israel. "Judge rightly," Samuel surely told them. But they did not. They did not love God's ways like Samuel did. The people knew this.

"You're old, Samuel," the people said, "and your sons are not good men. So give us a king to lead us." This made Samuel sad, so he prayed. "They are not turning their backs on you, Samuel," God told him. "They are turning their backs on Me."

God told Samuel to give the people a king but to warn them that a king would rule over them in ways they would not like. "We do not care!" they said. "We want a king!" So God told Samuel to anoint as king a man named Saul. Saul started off full of God's power but later turned away from Him. And Samuel was sad once again. "How long will you cry over Saul?" God asked Samuel. "Fill your horn with oil and go to Bethlehem. I have chosen a new king."

Samuel arrived in Bethlehem and, as God guided him, invited a man named Jesse, along with his sons, to come to a sacrifice with him. Samuel was very impressed with Jesse's son, Eliab and thought, *Surely this is who God has chosen.* But God said, "I am not impressed with the outside of a man, Samuel. I look at the man's heart."

Samuel met each of Jesse's sons – Abinadab was next in line. "This one, Lord?" Samuel asked. "No," God answered. Then Shammah. "This one?" Again, the Lord answered, "No." One by one each of Jesse's sons who were with him there passed in front of Samuel and each time one passed him God said, "No, not him." "Are these all the sons you have?" Samuel asked Jesse. "There's one more," Jesse answered. "My youngest, David, is taking care of the sheep."

When David arrived, God told Samuel: "Rise and anoint him with oil. He is the one I have chosen." From that day on the Spirit of the Lord came upon David in power.

David Fights Goliath

1 Samuel 17

One day, David's father sent him to take food to his brothers who were on the battlefield. As David was greeting his brothers, a giant named Goliath stepped out and made the same challenge he had been shouting at the Israelites for the past forty days. "Send a man to come and fight me!" Goliath roared. "If he beats me, we will be your slaves, but if I beat him, you will become our slaves." As usual, the Israelite soldiers saw Goliath and ran away to hide.

But David did not.

"Who is this man who mocks the armies of the living God?" he asked. David's oldest brother, Eliab, heard him ask this and got angry at him. "Why are you even here?" he sneered. "And who's taking care of your tiny flock of sheep?" Eliab goaded him, no doubt laughing as he said it. "You are just a cocky kid hoping to see a fight!"

Soon David was standing in front of King Saul explaining himself. "Do not give up hope," David said. "I will fight this man." King Saul looked at David, sizing him up, "You cannot fight Goliath. He is a mighty warrior and you are just a kid." David told King Saul, "Once a bear stole one of my sheep. I chased it down, struck it and saved the sheep from its mouth. I did the same thing when a lion attacked my flock - and when the lion tried to get me, I grabbed it by its mane, hit it and killed it." David stood up tall and added, "I killed a bear and a lion and I will kill this Goliath because he has insulted the armies of the living God. God delivered me from those animals and He will deliver me from this giant, too." King Saul was impressed. "Go, and God be with you."

King Saul put his own armor on David – a breastplate and helmet – and gave him his sword. David tried walking around with them on. "I cannot go in these." Instead, David found five smooth stones from the stream, put them in his shepherd's bag, pulled out his sling and walked towards Goliath.

Goliath looked at the boy David, ruddy and handsome, and got so mad his neck bulged as if it was going to pop. "I'll feed you to the birds and the beasts!" But David was not the least bit scared. "You come at me with a sword and a spear, but I come in the name of the Lord Almighty! This is God's battle and He will win it!"

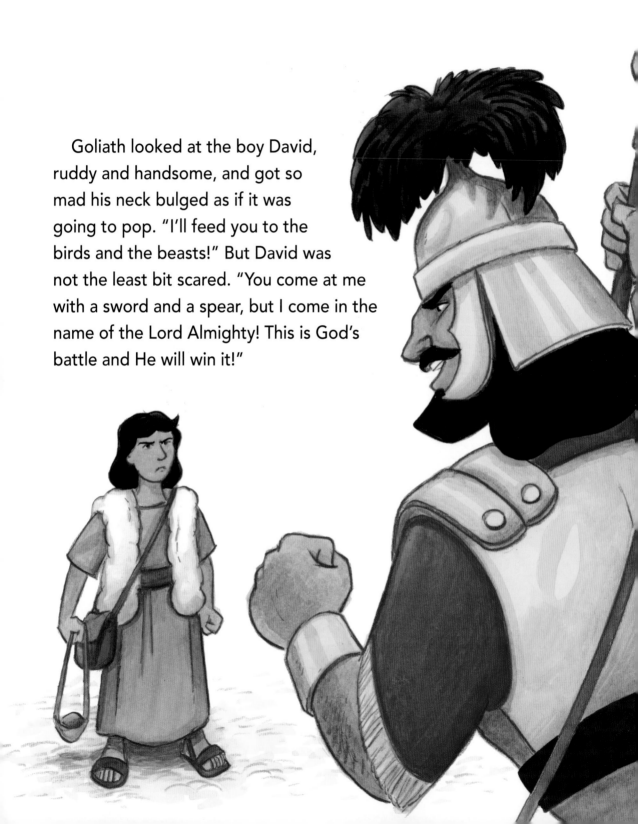

Goliath's lips snarled and his eyes narrowed as he moved to attack David who was running full speed at him. As David ran towards Goliath, he reached into his bag, pulled out a stone and slung it at the giant, hitting him in the forehead. Goliath fell to the ground with a thud that shook the whole Philistine army. David had killed Goliath in the power of the Lord.

Wise King Solomon

1 Kings 3

After David died, his son, Solomon, became king of Israel. Being king was a big job and Solomon knew he would need God's help. The Lord appeared to Solomon in a dream and said, "Ask for whatever you want me to give you." Solomon told the Lord, "I am so young and I do not know how to be a king. Lord, please give me a wise and understanding heart so I can be a good king for Your great people."

Solomon's answer pleased God. "Since you did not ask for a long life or great riches for yourself, but, instead, asked for a wise and understanding heart, I will make you wiser than any king has ever been or will ever be." God added, "And I will give you things you did not ask for – riches and treasures and honor."

God gave King Solomon treasures upon treasures. Many were given to him by the Queen of Sheba who traveled from far away to test him with questions and to see if Solomon's wealth and wisdom were as great as she had heard they were. "Praise be to the Lord your God," she said. "You are even wiser than I had been told."

One day, two women came to Solomon. "She has my baby!" one woman screamed. "No, she is lying. This is my baby!" the other yelled back. And they argued back and forth, each claiming the baby was her own. *Who was the real mother?*, everyone wondered. But how could anyone know?

Solomon knew just what to do. "Bring me a sword!" he called to the guard. "Now, cut the baby in two and give each one half."

Immediately, the woman who was lying and had stolen the child because her own baby had died, said, "Yes! Yes! Cut the baby in two!" But the real mother, full of love for her little one, cried, "No! Please don't do that. Give her the baby so he will live."

Immediately, King Solomon knew who the real mother was. Her love had made it clear. "Give the baby to this one," King Solomon said. "She is the baby's true mother."

Elijah, the Ravens and the Widow

1 Kings 17

Like father, like son – at least, that was the case with King Omri and his son Ahab. When Omri was king, the Bible tells us that he did more evil and more sin than any man who was king before him. Once he died and his son, Ahab, became king of Israel, Ahab did even worse. King Ahab married a woman named Jezebel and built a temple to her make-believe god called Baal and decided to serve Baal instead of the Lord.

One day, God sent his messenger Elijah to King Ahab with a message: "As the Lord lives, it will not rain nor will there even be dew on the ground for the next few years." God wanted to get Ahab's attention to turn his heart back to Him, but Ahab got angry at Elijah instead.

"Go," God told Elijah. "Hide near the brook." Elijah did and God sent ravens carrying food to him to take care of him and gave him clean water from the brook. When the brook dried up, because it had not rained in a very long time, God sent Elijah to stay with a poor widow and her son.

"Would you bring me a little water?" Elijah asked her. "And, please, a piece of bread?" "I have no bread," the widow woman told him. "I am about to use the last of my flour and oil to make a final meal for my son and me before we die." "Do not be afraid," Elijah told her. "Make me bread first, then make bread for you and your son. God will make your flour and oil feed you until He sends rain again." She believed Elijah and cooked food for them.

God did what Elijah promised He would do: God made her tiny bit of flour and her little jug of oil last and last and never run out.

Elijah and the Prophets of Baal
1 Kings 18:16-39

Elijah stayed at the widow's house for some time. It had been more than three long years since God sent rain on the land. Everything was dying. "Go," God told Elijah. "Go to King Ahab and I will send rain again." So Elijah went.

"You are the cause of Israel's troubles," King Ahab told Elijah. "I am not the cause," Elijah said. "You are. You have turned your back on God and followed fake gods. Bring all the Israelites to Mount Carmel – and bring all your false prophets and priests of your phony gods, too."

When all the people arrived, Elijah told them: "Make your choice. If the Lord is God, follow Him. If Baal is God, follow him." Then Elijah told them to stack wood into a pile, but to not light it, and to put two bulls on it. "Let's see who answers – Baal or the Lord," Elijah told them. "The god who answers by fire – he is God."

The prophets of Baal called out to their phony god from morning till noon but there was no answer and there was no fire.

"Maybe he is asleep," Elijah laughed. "Shout louder and wake him up."

The prophets of Baal danced and jumped and shouted and shrieked till evening but still there was no answer from Baal and there was no fire.

"Maybe he's out of town," Elijah mocked. "Maybe he's too busy!"

No matter what the prophets of Baal did, there was no answer and not even the tiniest puff of smoke.

Then Elijah built an altar to the Lord and dug a trench around it. "Soak the wood with water," Elijah told them. And they did. "Pour more water on it," Elijah said. And they did. "Soak it a third time," Elijah added. Now there was so much water on it, it filled the whole trench.

"Lord," Elijah prayed, "Show these people Your power so that they will love You again."

Suddenly, fire fell and burned up the bull, the wood, the stones, the water and even the dirt around the altar. When the people saw it, they worshipped God again.

Queen Esther

Esther 2; 5-7

Xerxes, king of Persia, hosted a big party. Everyone – from the least to the greatest - was there. "Bring my lovely Queen Vashti here," Xerxes told his servants. "I want everyone to see how beautiful she is." But Queen Vashti refused to come. Xerxes was furious.

"She what?!" one of his nobles gasped.

"Tell me it isn't so!" another official snorted.

"The nerve!" somebody else added, shocked.

"You must punish her for this behavior," one of the king's advisors insisted. Xerxes agreed. "Choose a new queen to replace her," they told him. And Xerxes did.

Xerxes' servants gathered beautiful women from all over the country and brought them to the palace to be pampered, primped and perfected with one full year of beauty treatments and a special diet. One young woman won the hearts of the king's trainers and Xerxes himself: Esther.

Esther was raised by her cousin, Mordecai. He loved her as if she were his own daughter. Mordecai paced near the courtyard to hear how Esther was doing. "Do not tell anyone you are a Jew," Mordecai told her. So Esther kept this a secret, obeying him just as she had done as a child. That is, until Haman's evil plan was revealed.

Haman was one of King Xerxes' chief officials. "Bow to this man," Xerxes commanded. But Mordecai would not bow to Haman – only to God. When Haman saw this, he was enraged. "I will kill him," Haman vowed, "and I will kill all of Mordecai's people – the Jews – who live in Xerxes' kingdom!"

When Mordecai learned of Haman's plan, he tore his clothes, put on sackcloth and ashes, and walked through the city streets wailing and

crying bitterly – and all the Jews in the kingdom did the same. "Go find out what Mordecai is upset about," Queen Esther told her servant. The servant did and Mordecai told him all about Haman's evil plan. "Esther must talk to the king about this," Mordecai said. "She must plead for our safety."

Esther sent her servant back to Mordecai with this frightening message: "No one can go to the king without an invitation. To do so, is to die – unless the king lowers his gold scepter and spares that person's life." Mordecai weighed the servant's words carefully. "Tell the queen this," he began, "Perhaps God has given you your royal position for this very reason." Esther knew Mordecai was right. "Tell all the Jews to fast for three days," Esther said. "I will fast, too. Then I will go to the king, even though it is against his law. And if I die trying, so be it."

God gave Esther favor with the king. He lowered his gold scepter, invited her in and listened to all she told him. "Who made up this horrible plan?" Xerxes asked Esther. "Haman did," she answered. The king was furious. Xerxes helped saved the Jews and ordered his soldiers to hang Haman on the gallows Haman had hoped to hang Mordecai on.

Shadrach, Meshach & Abednego
Daniel 3

Some kings adorn themselves in their most regal robes, decorate themselves with fancy rings and necklaces, polish their jewel-studded crowns and scepter then strike a commanding pose on their royal throne while a great artist paints a masterpiece of them. King Nebuchadnezzar had a statue of gold made of himself – a ninety feet tall gold statue!

"When the music starts," King Nebuchadnezzar's servant announced to all, "bow down and worship this statue. If you don't, you'll burn in the furnace." The musicians played, the people bowed, the king was happy – that is, until he saw Shadrach, Meshach and Abednego standing.

Maybe the king had forgotten how much he liked these three young men and how he had questioned them and found them to be ten times wiser than the other young men in his kingdom. Not likely.

Maybe the king had forgotten how these three young men, along with their friend Daniel, prayed to their God and how their God had revealed his troubling dream to them – and the dream's meaning. Again, not likely.

Maybe King Nebuchadnezzar was simply acting too big for his britches.

"I will give you one last chance," King Nebuchadnezzar told them. "Bow or be thrown into the blazing furnace where no god can rescue you!"

The three stood firm and boldly said: "We do not need to defend ourselves. Our God is certainly able to save us from this fire – but even if He doesn't, we want you to know, that we will not serve your gods or worship this statue."

"Make the fire seven times hotter!" the king commanded. Then he told his strongest soldiers to tie them up. The fire was so hot, it instantly killed the soldiers as they pushed Shadrach, Meshach and Abednego into the furnace.

Just then, King Nebuchadnezzar leapt to his feet in amazement. "Look!" he shouted. "I see *four* men walking around in the fire! Untied! Unharmed! And the fourth looks like a son of the gods!" The king crept close to the furnace and shouted, "Shadrach, Meshach and Abednego, servants of the Most High God, come out! Come out!" And when they did, the king saw that not a single hair was burnt nor did their clothes have the faintest smell of smoke.

The King shouted: "Praise be to the God of Shadrach, Meshach and Abednego, who has sent His angel and rescued His servants! No other God can save this way!"

Daniel in the Lions' Den
Daniel 6

Being a good worker brings many rewards. Daniel knew this well. When King Darius took over the kingdom of Babylon, he put 120 governors in charge of different areas. Then King Darius put three administrators in charge of the 120 governors. Of these three administrators, King Darius was most impressed with Daniel. Indeed, the king was so pleased with Daniel that he decided to put him in charge of his whole kingdom. And that brings me to my second point: being a good worker sometimes brings you a little trouble – especially when the people around you are jealous, dishonest and evil.

"We have got to find a way to get Daniel into trouble," they decided. "Let's spy on him. The minute we find him doing something wrong, we will arrest him and then he will be out of our way."

So they watched Daniel closely. They hid behind pillars. They sneakily listened in on his conversations. They peeked through his important documents. But they could not find anything but good in Daniel.

"It's useless!" one of them whined.

"Pointless!" another chimed in.

"A total waste of time!" still another added.

"Yeh," one of them sighed. "If only praying were a crime," he sneered. "Then we could lock him up and throw away the key! That guy prays to his God three times a day!"

"That's it!" one of them snapped. "That is how we will get him! We will make a law that makes it a crime to pray to anyone but to King Darius himself!"

And that's just what they did. In no time at all, they caught Daniel praying to God as he always had done.

"O King Darius," one of them said, "we have found a man breaking your new law. He does not pray to you, O King, so you must throw him into the lions' den like your new law says."

"Yes, yes," the king agreed. "That is the law and it must be followed."

"The lawbreaker is Daniel," they told him.

This caused King Darius much stress and he spent the rest of the day trying to find a way to save Daniel but could not. "Daniel," King Darius said, "may your God, whom you serve wholeheartedly, rescue you." They put Daniel in the lions' den and closed the door.

The king was so upset he could not eat or sleep all night, and when the first light of morning broke, King Darius raced to the lions' den and called, "Daniel, servant of the living God, has your God saved you from the lions?" And to King Darius's great joy and relief, he heard Daniel answer. "O King, my God sent His angel, and He shut the mouths of the lions."

King Darius was overjoyed. "Lift Daniel out of there now!" he commanded. Not only that, King Darius ordered that the ones who brought these false charges be thrown into the lions' den – and they were.

Then King Darius made a new law: "I decree that everyone in my kingdom must honor and praise the God of Daniel."

The New Testament

Baby Jesus Is Born!

Luke 1:26-2:20

Zechariah was a priest in Israel. One day, when he was in the temple, an angel appreared to him. "Do not be afraid," Gabriel said. "Your wife Elizabeth will have a son. Name him 'John'. He will get people ready to meet the Savior of the world."

Later, Gabriel appeared to a young girl named Mary. "Greetings!" he said. Mary was startled, too. "Do not be afraid, Mary," Gabriel said. "God wants you to be the mother of the Savior of the world." Mary was confused. "But I am not married." "Nothing is impossible for God," Gabriel said. "God will put the baby in your womb."

In time, Zechariah and Elizabeth's baby boy was born. They named him 'John' just as Gabriel had told them to do. Everyone was thrilled for them for they had wanted a baby for many, many years.

When the time was drawing near for Mary's baby to be born, she and Joseph (her husband-to-be) had to make a long journey from their hometown of Nazareth to the town of Bethlehem. While they were in Bethlehem, Mary's baby was born. She wrapped him in cloths and gently layed him in a manger they used for a bed.

Just outside Bethlehem, where shepherds were watching their sheep, an angel appeared in the sky and the glory of heaven shone around them. The shepherds were afraid. "Do not be afraid," the angel told them. "I have great news! Christ the Lord has been born today! You will find Him lying in a manger." Suddenly, the sky was filled with angels! They were praising God, saying: "Glory to God in the highest, and peace to all the people on earth!" Then they disappeared as mysteriously as they had appeared.

The shepherds found baby Jesus just as the angels had said. And they praised God, too!

Wise Men Visit Jesus

Matthew 2:1-12

The birth of Jesus was big news. So big it was announced by its own special star. Wise men from the East saw this star and knew it marked the arrival of a very special baby – a baby king. They came to Jerusalem to worship this new King. "Where is the One who has been born King of the Jews?" they asked.

When King Herod heard about the wise men and learned what they were saying, he was so upset he was shaking. He gathered all the Jewish chief priests and teachers of the law and asked them: "Where is this 'King', this Messiah, supposed to be born?" The priests and teachers knew right away. "In Bethlehem," they told him. "Just as the prophet Micah promised."

Later, King Herod met with the wise men secretly. "Tell me," he whispered, "when did this star you have told me about first appear?" After that, he told them: "Go, look everywhere until you find the child. Then, once you have found Him, come back and tell me. I would like to worship Him, too." (But this was a lie. King Herod did not want to worship the baby. Instead, he wanted to kill Him).

The wise men saw the star once again and followed it until it stopped over the place where Jesus was. They went into the house, saw the child with His mother, Mary, and bowed down and worshipped Him. Not only that, they gave Him treasures and presented Him with gold, frankincense and myrrh. And, after being warned in a dream not to go back to Herod, they returned to their country by another way.

The Boy Jesus
Luke 2:41-52

When Jesus was twelve years old, He went with His parents to Jerusalem. This was something they did every year to celebrate the Feast of the Passover. The Feast of the Passover is a special celebration when Jews remember how God used Moses to save them from their long slavery in Egypt many, many years ago.

After it was over, Mary and Joseph began their long journey back
home. Some time late in the day, after many miles of walking, they began
looking for Jesus among the group. I suppose their questions were asked
calmly at first as they felt sure He was simply walking with His friends.

"Have you seen Jesus?" Mary likely asked one of the boys in the caravan. "No, ma'am."

"Is Jesus with you?" Joseph, no doubt, asked another. "I have not seen Him all day," might have been the reply.

Soon, they realized He was not anywhere in the group and that they have no idea where He might be. *Did He fall behind the group? Is He out there somewhere all by Himself? Alone? Tired? Hungry? Hurt?*

Mary and Joseph hurriedly retraced their steps all the way back to Jerusalem. They looked everywhere for Him – asking anyone who might be able to help: "Have you seen our boy?"

After three days, they finally found Him. Jesus was in the temple, sitting among the teachers, listening and asking questions and amazing everyone with His understanding and His answers. He was not lost. He was not tired or scared or hungry or hurt. He was right where He felt He ought to be.

"Son," His mother asked Him, shocked and dumbfounded. "Why have You treated us this way? We have been searching everywhere for You."

"Did you not know I had to be here in My Father's house?" Jesus answered them, true as an arrow and with kindness. His answer baffled His parents, but His mother never forgot it. She treasured it.

Jesus returned home with them and obeyed them.

John Baptizes Jesus
Matthew 3

John the Baptist was preaching out in the Desert of Judea. God sent John to tell the people that Jesus was coming. John's clothes were made of camel's hair and he wore a leather belt around his waist. Guess what he ate? Locusts and wild honey. Yummy!

"Change for the good!" John said. "Be sorry for your sins and obey God. The Savior of the world is coming! Get ready!"

"What do we need to do?" the people asked.

"Share with one another," John told them. "Take care of one another. If you have two coats, give one of your coats to someone who does not have one. Same with food," John said. "Share your food with those who are hungry and do not have food to eat."

Some tax collectors asked him, "What do we need to do?"

"Do not cheat people," he said. "Do not trick them into paying more taxes than they owe."

"What about us?" some soldiers asked.

"Do not lie about people to get them into trouble," he said. "Do not bully people either. And stop complaining about your pay."

Many listened to John, confessed their sins and were baptized by John in the Jordan River.

One day Jesus came and was baptized by John, too. When Jesus came up out of the water, He saw the Spirit of God in the form of a dove come rest on His shoulder and He heard God speaking to Him from heaven.

"This is My Son," God said. "I love Him. He pleases Me completely."

Jesus Is Tempted in the Desert

Luke 4:1-13

Jesus spent forty days and nights in the desert without eating anything. Of course, he became very hungry. Just then, the tempter came to him and said, "If you are the Son of God, tell these stones to become bread."

But Jesus told him, "God's Word says, 'Man does not live on bread only, but on every word God speaks'."

The tempter then took Jesus to a very high mountain. In an instant, he showed Jesus all the kingdoms of the world and all of their power and glory. "This is all mine," the tempter told Him. "I can give it to anyone I want to. If you will bow down and worship me, I will give them all to You."

But Jesus told him, "God's Word says, 'Worship the Lord your God and serve Him only!'"

The tempter took Jesus to Jerusalem, to the temple, and stood Him on the highest point. "If you are the Son of God," he said. "Jump! God's Word says 'He will send angels to guard You and hold You so that You won't get hurt at all.'"

But Jesus told him, "God's Word says 'Do not put God to the test.' No, go away!"

The tempter left Jesus alone (at least, for a while) and angels came and helped Jesus.

Jesus Heals

Luke 8:40-56

One day Jairus, a synagogue official, pushed his way through the large crowd surrounding Jesus. When he got to Jesus, he fell at Jesus' feet, and begged Him: "Please," he cried, "please come and save my daughter. She's dying but I know You can heal her." So Jesus went with him and started towards Jairus's house, but the crowd pressed in on them as they walked. Many were calling out to Jesus, hoping He would heal them, too.

A woman was there who had spent all of her money trying to get well. Year after year, doctor after doctor and still, no one could cure her sickness. Instead of getting better, she got worse. When she heard about Jesus, she believed He could heal her. In fact, she believed that if she could only touch the hem of His clothes, she would be as good as new. So, just like Jairus, she worked her way through the crowd until she was close enough to touch Him. She was right! She was healed the moment she touched His clothes.

Suddenly, Jesus stopped walking. "Who touched My clothes?" He asked the crowd. His followers were baffled. *How can He ask who touched Him? Everybody's bumping into everybody!* "Lord," one of them asked, "in a crowd like this, how can you ask such a thing?" But Jesus studied the faces of the people around Him.

The woman fell at His feet and trembling with fear told Him her whole story. Jesus loved hearing about her faith and courage. "Your faith has healed you," He told her. Just then, some friends of Jairus showed up. "Jairus," they said, tenderly, "your daughter is dead. Why bother Jesus with it anymore?" But Jesus said, "Do not be afraid; just believe."

Jesus went into the room where Jairus's daughter was, held her hand and said, "Little girl, get up." Immediately, she got up. Jesus had healed her, too.

Jesus Calms the Waters
Matthew 8:23-27

Jesus was a wonderful storyteller, a kind healer and an amazing teacher. Jesus also had power over the winds and the waves and the water.

One time, Jesus and His followers got into a boat and headed off for another town. Suddenly, a huge storm came up. It rocked the boat from side to side. It lifted the boat up and down. The waves were so big they swept over the boat, one after another.

Jesus' followers were terrified. No doubt they did all they could to hang on and hang in, but their strength was surely getting weak. Worse than that, their fears were getting stronger. Soon they were in sheer panic, thinking they were about to drown.

Was Jesus afraid? Not at all. In fact, He was peacefully asleep – right in the middle of a violent storm.

With eyes as big as their fishing nets and shouting at the top of their voices, they went to Jesus and woke Him up. "Lord, save us!" they cried. "Before we drown!"

Jesus woke up, looked at them and said, "Why are you all shaking with fear? Trust God!" Then He got up and told the wind and the waves to be calm and they obeyed. The wind stopped whipping them around and the waves seemed to lie down as if taking a sudden and peaceful afternoon nap.

Jesus' followers were amazed and asked one another, "What kind of man is this? He speaks to the wind and waves and water - and they do what He says!"

Feeding the Five Thousand

Matthew 14:13-21

Big things were happening.

Crippled people were able to walk. Jesus healed their legs.

Deaf people were able to hear. Jesus healed their ears.

Blind people were able to see. Jesus healed their eyes.

Sick people got well. Jesus healed them, too!

For three days the big, big crowd followed Jesus.

They listened to Him teach about God.

Their eyes got big when they watched Jesus heal someone.

Now they were hungry. Big growls came from everyone's tummy.

"Let's feed everyone," Jesus said.

Philip's eyes must have gotten wide.

"Lord, it would cost big, big bucks to feed all these people," Philip told Jesus.

Andrew wanted to help. "This boy has five small loaves of bread and two tiny fish," Andrew told Jesus. "It will not feed very many."

Jesus had a big lesson to teach His helpers.

"Tell the people to sit down," Jesus told him. "We are going to eat."

The people sat down on the comfy green grass. They did not know it, but they were about to join Jesus in a picnic.

Jesus took the loaves of bread and said a prayer to thank God for it.

Jesus' helpers gave bread to all the people - as much as they wanted to eat! There was plenty!

Jesus took the two small fish and thanked God again.

Every person there ate as much fish as they wanted.

Big hairy hungry men ate all they wanted.
Small ladies ate their fill.
And every little child got plenty to eat, too!
There were even leftovers!
"Gather up what is left," Jesus told His helpers.
They filled up twelve big baskets!
Talk about big memories!
God does big amazing things!

Jesus Walks on Water

Matthew 14:22-36

One time, after a long day of teaching and healing, Jesus told His followers to get into their boat and head off to the other side of the lake. After that, Jesus sent all of the people home who had gathered to hear Him or meet Him or be healed by Him that day. Then Jesus climbed up a mountain and prayed until very late in the night.

After he finished praying, He began walking - *on the water* -
out to the boat to meet His followers. It was dark and in the middle
of the night – about four in the morning! "Look!" one of them screamed
in fear. "It's a ghost!" Soon they were all shaking.

"Do not be afraid," Jesus called to them. "It is Me!"

Peter leaned out over the boat, squinted his eyes to see better. "Lord,
if it's You," Peter said, "tell me to come to You on the water." Jesus
probably smiled, then said, "Come on, Peter."

Caught up in the marvel of it all, Peter could not take his eyes off of Jesus as he got out of the boat, put his foot flat on the water and began to walk on it! How many steps did Peter take? One? Three? Fifty? It's impossible to say but one thing we do know is this: Peter walked on the water until he thought about the winds and waves and allowed fear to take over his mind.

"Lord!" Peter cried as he began to sink. "Save me!"

Immediately, Jesus grabbed him. "Why did you doubt, Peter?" Jesus asked him. They climbed into the boat, the wind died down, and all of Jesus' followers in the boat worshiped Jesus and said, "You are the Son of God!"

And, of course, they were right.

The Good Samaritan

Luke 10:25-37

One time a very religious man asked Jesus, "What must I do to live forever with God?" He did not ask Jesus to learn. Instead, he asked to see if Jesus understood God's Word like he did.

"Tell me what God's Word says about this?" Jesus asked him back. No doubt showing off a bit, he answered, "Love God with all your heart, soul, strength and mind. And love your neighbor as yourself."

"That is right," Jesus told him. "Do this and you will live."

But the man wanted to prove that he was doing everything right and had no need to change his behavior, so he asked, "And exactly *who* is my neighbor?" In other words, who do I *have* to love and who can I ignore?

So Jesus told him a story. "A man went on a trip and was beat up and robbed by thieves. Then the robbers stole his clothes and left him to die on the dirty road.

A priest walked by, saw the man, and, instead of stopping to help, switched to the opposite side of the road and walked on by.

A Levite passed by, too. He also saw the hurt man but, instead of helping, switched to the opposite side of the road and walked on by as well.

Then a Samaritan came by. He saw the man, felt sorry for him, bandaged up his wounds and helped him every way he could. Then, instead of leaving the man there, he put him on his donkey, took him to an inn and took care of him. The next day, he gave the innkeeper money to take care of the man until he returned from his trip."

The religious man probably did not like Jesus' story very much because he probably did not like Samaritans. And yet, Jesus made the Samaritan the hero.

"Which man was the true neighbor to the hurt man?" Jesus asked. The religious man had to admit, "The one who took care of him."

"That is right," Jesus said. "Go and do the same."

Jesus Raises Lazarus from the Dead
John 11:1-44

One time, while Jesus was in another town, someone told him: "Lord, the one I love is sick." Jesus said, "This sickness will not end in death. This sickness is for God's glory so that God's Son might be glorified through it."

Two days later, Jesus said, "Let us go back to Judea." His followers protested, saying, "But Teacher, some people there just tried to stone You. Do you really want to go back?" "Our friend Lazarus is dead. I am going to do something to help you believe in Me." Then Thomas spoke courageously, "Yes, let's go with Him even if it means our death."

Martha ran to Jesus. "Lord, if you had only been here, my brother would not have died." Jesus said, "Lazarus will rise again." Martha agreed. "I know he will in the resurrection at the Last Day." Jesus looked in her eyes and told her, "I am the resurrection and the life. Whoever believes in Me will live – even though he dies; and whoever lives and believes Me is free of death's grip forever. Do you believe this?" "Yes, I do," she said. "You are the Savior of the world. You are God's Son."

Mary ran to Jesus and fell at His feet. Jesus saw her tears and the tears of all who were crying with her and said, "Where have you laid him?" "Come," they said. Jesus was so deeply moved, He cried, too.

"Move the stone from the grave," Jesus told them. "But, Lord," Martha said, "He's been dead four days. It will stink." Jesus said, "Did I not tell you, if you believed, God would show His glory?"

They took away the stone. Jesus prayed, "Father, thank You for always hearing Me. I want these people to believe that You sent Me." Then Jesus shouted, "Come out, Lazarus!" And Lazarus – wrapped up like a mummy - came back to life and walked outside. Many of Mary's friends saw and believed in Jesus.

The Transfiguration of Jesus
Matthew 17:1-13

An amazing thing happened to Jesus that only three of His closest followers were allowed to see. Jesus took Peter, James and John up a high mountain. Once there, they were very sleepy but something happened that woke them straight up. Jesus began to look very different!

His face became as bright as the sun and His clothes as bright as a lightning flash! Then two men, Moses and Elijah, appeared in a glorious display with Jesus and began talking with Him. They spoke about something that was going to happen to Jesus very soon.

Peter, James and John were terrified. "Lord," Peter said, not really knowing what to say, "It's good for us to be here. I can make up three shelters for You and Elijah and Moses, if You'd like me to."

Just then, a bright cloud appeared and covered them like a blanket - which frightened them even more – and they heard a voice say: "This is my Son, whom I love. Listen to Him."

They were so scared. They fell face first to the ground. Jesus came to them, touched them and said, "Get up. Do not be afraid." And when they looked up, Elijah and Moses were gone.

As they were walking down the mountain, Jesus said, "Do not talk about this to anyone until after the Son of Man has been raised from the dead." So they did not tell anyone; but they did not understand what Jesus meant by "raised from the dead."

Soon, they – and all of the world with them – would understand it completely.

The Forgiven Man Who Would Not Forgive

Matthew 18:21-35

Jesus not only *wants* us to forgive others, He says we *must*. That's how heaven works.

One time Peter asked Jesus, "Lord, how many times should I forgive someone who does me wrong? Seven?" Jesus told him, "No, but seventy times seven." Then Jesus told them a story about a man who had been forgiven but did not forgive others.

"One day," Jesus said, "a king decided to sort out who owed him what and what to do about it. A man who owed the king several million dollars was brought before the king. Since the man was not able to pay what he owed, the king ordered that he and his wife and their children and all the things he owned be sold to repay the debt.

"The servant dropped to his knees and begged the king to give him more time. 'Please,' the man cried, 'please, be patient and I'll pay you everything I owe you.' The king felt sorry for the man. He told him, 'I am not going to make you pay me back. Go,' he said, 'I have erased your debt.'

"No doubt relieved, the servant went out and found one of his own servants, grabbed him and began to choke him. 'You owe me three dollars!' he shouted. 'Pay me back right now!'

"'Please, oh, please,' the servant begged him, 'be patient and I will pay you back.' But the wicked man said, 'No!' and he threw the poor man in jail. 'You'll stay in here until you've paid back every penny!' he yelled.

"The king heard about this and called the first man back to his palace. 'You wicked servant,' the king said. 'I erased your debt because you begged me to. Should you not have done the same thing? Should you not have shown this man mercy?'

"'Throw this wicked man in jail!' the king told his guards. 'And do not let him out until he has paid back every cent.'"

Jesus said, "This is how God will treat you if you do not forgive others fully and completely from your heart."

The Ten Lepers
Luke 17:11-19

Jesus healed many people – more than we will ever know! Here are just a few: He healed Peter's mother-in-law when she had a fever. He healed a crippled man. He healed a man with a shriveled hand. He healed a man who had been blind all of his life. He raised Lazarus from the dead!

One time, Jesus healed ten men at the same time. These men had a disease called leprosy. Back then, people believed you could easily catch leprosy if you got close to someone who had it.

"Jesus! Master!" they called out to Him from a long way off. "Have pity on us!"

"Go show yourselves to the priests," Jesus told them. Then, as they were walking to see the priests, they were healed. One of the ten saw his sores disappear and knew Jesus had healed them. He immediately stopped, turned around and went back to Jesus. He was so happy. He was shouting praises to God all the way back to Jesus and when he saw Jesus, he fell down at His feet and thanked Him.

"Were all ten of you not healed?" Jesus asked him. "Where are the other nine? Rise and go," Jesus told him. "Your faith had made you well."

The Pharisee and the Tax Collector

Luke 18:9-14

One day, Jesus was with some people who thought very highly of themselves. These people liked to pat themselves on the back and keep long lists of all the things they did right. More than that, they believed they were better than everybody else. Jesus decided to tell them a story about themselves.

"Two men went to the temple to pray. One was a Pharisee," Jesus added and, no doubt they thought to themselves: *Yes, yes, it is so great to be a Pharisee because we Pharisees are so good at being good and even better at being better than those who are not good.* "The other man was a tax collector," Jesus said. (I can almost hear them booing at the thought.)

"The Pharisee prayed like this: 'I thank you, God, that I am better than other men. I am very religious and I give you a little bit of my money, too – regularly! I thank You that I am not like this, this, this yucky, stinky tax collector.'" *Why not pray like this?* I can imagine them thinking. *Every line of the prayer was as true as true can be.* But Jesus was not finished with His story. "The tax collector could not even look up towards heaven, but, instead, bowed his head and said, 'God, have mercy on me. I'm such a sinner.'"

Then Jesus surprised them. "I tell you the truth, it was the tax collector and not the Pharisee who went home made right and at peace with God. For everyone who exalts himself will be humbled, and he who humbles himself will be exalted."

Jesus wants us to pray anywhere and everywhere about anything and everything, but when we pray Jesus wants us to pray with a deep and thankful love for God's great kindness to us. Treasuring God's love in our hearts keeps us from being bossy or rude or prideful or demanding and it makes our prayers pure and pleasing to our loving Creator.

Let the Children Come to Me

Matthew 19:13-15

Jesus loves people – all kinds of people. Big people. Little people. Men. Women. Sick people. Healthy people. Hairy people. Bald people. Loud people. Quiet people. Rich people. Poor people. People of every color and nation.

Did I mention Jesus loved old people and young people, too? Well, He certainly does. In fact, one time people were bringing little children and babies to Jesus so He would touch them and bless them and I am sure it made Jesus smile from ear to ear, but when Jesus' followers saw this happening, they decided to put an end to it at once.

"Move away! Move away!" I can almost hear them saying. "Shoo!"
It's as if they thought that kids and babies were a nuisance to the Savior,
or that Jesus was for grown-ups only. They were wrong and Jesus let
them know about it.

"Let the little children come to Me," Jesus told them firmly. "Do
not stop them. The kingdom of God belongs to them." Jesus leaned
in closer and looked His followers in the eye, then added: "I tell you
the truth, if you do not come to God like a child does, you will never
understand Him at all."

Then Jesus gathered the children around Him again and hugged and
blessed them.

The Prodigal Son

Luke 15:11-32

Jesus loved to teach people about God. He most often taught by telling stories. When He wanted people to know how much God loved them, He told them a story about a boy who grew up and left his father's home. "Father," the boy said, "give me my inheritance." So the father did.

Soon, the boy took all the money his dad gave him and went off to a faraway country. The boy spent all the money on foolish and wild living and soon hadn't a penny to his name. To make things worse, the whole country was starving, too.

The boy finally got a man to give him a job feeding his pigs. Do you know that things got so bad for the boy and that he got so hungry he would have gladly eaten right beside the pigs out of the trough?

Well, that was a bit of a wake-up call for him. "In my father's house," he said to himself, "even the servants have leftovers and yet, here I am starving!" He thought about it for a second, then stood up and said, "I am going home." But as he walked, he remembered how he had demanded his money and, worse, how he spent it. He knew he did many things his father would not be proud of. "I am no longer worthy of being called his son," he thought. "I will tell him that I am sorry and that I have sinned." The boy continued home, hoping his dad would hire him as a worker.

Jesus said, "While the boy was still a long way off, his father saw him and his heart was full of love for him." And that the father did not wait for the boy to grovel his way up to the porch, but instead "ran to his son, threw his arms around him and kissed him." As the boy tried to apologize for all the bad things he had done, the father shouted, "Quick! Put my best robe on him! And a ring for his hand! And sandals for his feet! Let us have a feast and celebrate! For this boy of mine was lost and is now found!"

And that, Jesus said, is what God is like.

Jesus Loved to Pray

Mark 1:35-39

Jesus loved to talk with God. Sometimes He would wake up early in the morning, before the sun came up, go off to a private place and pray to God. (Mark 1:35) Sometimes Jesus prayed all night long. Wow! (Luke 6:12)

What do we pray? Here are some things Jesus says to pray about:

"Pray for those who mistreat you because God is good to those who are mean to Him." (Matthew 5:44-48 & Luke 6:28)

"Do not pray just so others will see you praying and think you are amazing. Pray to really talk with God, not to be seen by others." (Matthew 6:5)

"Pray to God for strength to do what is right when you are tempted to do wrong." (Luke 22:40)

What else does the Bible teach me about praying?

"Pray about everything!" (Philippians 4:6)

"Pray for others." (2 Thessalonians 1:11)

"Pray when you are in trouble." (James 5:13)

"Pray all the time!" (1 Thessalonians 5:17)

Zacchaeus

Luke 19:1-10

Everywhere Jesus went, people followed – lots of people. Sometimes there were so many people crowding around Jesus that it was hard to even get close enough to get a good look at Him – especially if you were short like Zacchaeus.

A crowd gathered around Jesus as soon as He entered Jericho. Can you see little Zacchaeus trying to work his way to the front of the crowd? "Excuse me please," he might have said while tapping a tall man on the shoulder. "Pardon me!" he may have whispered to a band of soldiers. "Coming through," he likely announced to another patch of people, hoping they would move aside and let him by, but nobody did. No matter how much he hopped or how high he jumped, he could not see Jesus.

Suddenly, he had an idea. He decided to race up the road, ahead of the crowd, and wait for Jesus to pass by there. Then – to make sure he got a good view – he climbed up in a tree.

When Jesus reached the place where Zacchaeus was waiting, He called him by name. "Zacchaeus," Jesus said. "Hurry! Come down from there. I must go to your house today." Zacchaeus was thrilled and climbed down at once, but many in the crowd did not like it.

"Jesus is going to Zacchaeus's house?" they grumbled. "Does He not know Zacchaeus is a greedy, cheating, tax collector? Does Jesus not know that Zacchaeus bullies people's money away from them, stuffs his pockets until he's rich, and sends the rest as taxes to Caesar?" They could not understand why Jesus would be kind to someone so, well, unkind. "Does Jesus not know what type of a man Zacchaeus is?" they wondered. And, of course, Jesus did.

I am sure it felt to Zacchaeus that everyone around him hated him – everyone, that is, except Jesus. Jesus loved him, was kind to him, called him by name, went to his house. And that love turned Zacchaeus's world inside-out.

"Look, Lord!" Zacchaeus shouted. "Right here and now, I give half of all my things to the poor! And I will pay the money back to everyone I have cheated – in fact, I will pay them four times more than what I took!"

Jesus was so happy. He said, no doubt while laughing with delight, "Today salvation has come to this house!"

The Poor Widow's Offering
Mark 12:41-44

One day, Jesus sat down on the other side of the temple's treasury box and watched. There was quite a crowd gathered. Each person, in his turn, approached the box, dropped their offering money into it and went on their way.

One man pulled out a large purse, reached in, jingled the coins around noisily, held the shiny coins high above his head and then, with an impressive display of his arms, dropped the coins into the treasury box – making sure they'd clank against the side of it.

Another man, fancily dressed in a priestly robe and adorned with gold rings on nearly every finger, dropped his coins into the treasury box next.

More followed. At times, it almost seemed like they were having a contest to see whose offering got the biggest *oohs* and *ahhhs* from the crowd of onlookers.

Finally, a feeble old woman, dusty, plain and poor, quietly made her way to the treasury box. She took out two tiny coins which, together, added up to less than a penny. She slipped them into the treasury box then went on her way.

Jesus called His followers to Him and said, "I tell you the truth, that poor widow has put more into the treasury than all the others." Perhaps the followers wondered if Jesus had noticed all the others – especially the rich folks who had dropped in so much. But, of course, Jesus had noticed them. "They all gave out of their extra," Jesus explained, "but this woman has given the only money she had left in the world."

Jesus Washes His Followers' Feet
John 13:1-17

Jesus knew it was time for Him to die and go back to God. He gathered His closest followers together for a special dinner. He got up from the table, took off His cloak, and wrapped a towel around His waist. Then He poured water into a bowl and started washing His followers' feet and drying them with the towel.

"No, Lord," Peter said, "You should not be washing our feet like this." Peter knew that washing feet was a job usually done by the lowliest of servants and not someone as important as Jesus.

"You do not understand yet what I am doing," Jesus said, "but you will later."

Jesus washed each of His followers' feet and then sat back down. "You call Me 'Teacher' and you call Me 'Lord' and that's good to do because that's what I am," Jesus told them. "And I – your Lord and Teacher – have shown you what you should do for one another. You should wash each other's feet."

After this, Jesus was troubled in His heart. "Someone here is going to turn against Me. The one I give this piece of bread to." Then Jesus dipped it in a dish and handed it to Judas. "Do what you are about to do quickly," Jesus told Judas. Judas left that very moment and disappeared into the night to do the devil's deed of turning against Jesus.

Jesus Tells His Followers to Love One Another
John 13:31-38

After Judas left, Jesus told His followers He was about to go away. He meant that He was about to die and go back to God, but they did not understand that. "My children," he told them, "I will be with you only a little while longer. I give a new command: Love one another just as I have loved you. Everyone will know you are My followers if you will love one another."

Peter was confused. "Where are you going away to, Lord?"

"Where I am going, you cannot go now, Peter," Jesus told him. "But you will later."

"Lord," Peter urged Him, "why can't I follow you now? I will give up my own life for you!"

"Will you really, Peter?" Jesus asked Him. "I tell you the truth, you will turn against Me three times this very night – before the rooster crows." But Peter said, "Even if I have to die with you, Lord, I will never turn against you." And all of the other followers said the same.

"I am the way and the truth and the life," Jesus told them. "No one comes to God the Father unless they come to God through Me."

Jesus told them many more things that night. He told them to obey His commands and that that is how someone shows that they really love Jesus. He told them they were His friends and that God the Father loves them. Then Jesus prayed for them and for all of the people who would one day come to love Him – people like you!

Jesus Is Betrayed, Arrested and Abandoned

Mark 14:32-72

Jesus took His followers to a place called Gethsemane. He was very sad and prayed and prayed. "The hour has come," Jesus said to His followers who had fallen asleep. Here comes My betrayer."

Just then, Judas walked up to them. He was leading a large group of people and soldiers carrying torches, swords and sticks. Judas stepped close to Jesus and kissed Him on the cheek. "Judas," Jesus asked him, "do you betray with a kiss?" And, shamefully, he did.

They grabbed Jesus and arrested
Him. At this, Peter pulled out a sword and cut off
the right ear of the high priest's servant. "No more
of this!" Jesus said. Then He touched the man's
ear and healed him. "Put your sword away, Peter,"
Jesus told him. "Do you not know I could call on God and He would send
a multitude angels? But this has to happen. This is God's plan for Me."

Then Peter and all of Jesus' followers ran away leaving Jesus alone with the mob.

The crowd took Jesus to the high priest and Peter snuck along, far behind them. While one person after another lied about Jesus and hurt Him, Peter waited nearby. "You were with Jesus, too," a servant said. But Peter lied, "I do not know what you are talking about!"

Then another girl said, "This man was with Jesus." Again, Peter lied. "I do not know Jesus!"

Finally, someone else said, "You are certainly one of Jesus' followers." But Peter lied a third time. "I tell you I do not even know the man named Jesus!" Immediately, a rooster crowed and Peter remembered that Jesus had said this would happen.

Peter felt so ashamed. He cried and cried.

Jesus Is Crucified

Mark 15

Jesus was lied about, made fun of, mistreated and hurt all through the night. They pushed Him from Pilate's palace to Herod's and back to Pilate's again, begging them both to order that Jesus be put to death. But neither Pilate nor Herod found any reason to do so. "I will punish Him and then let Him go," Pilate told the angry mob, hoping that would take care of the matter, but they shouted louder and louder, "Crucify Him! Crucify Him!" until Pilate finally gave in to their demands.

The soldiers took Jesus and made Him carry His own heavy cross. They nailed Jesus' hands and feet to the cross and put Him between two criminals who were also being crucified.

"He saved others," someone sneered. "Let's see Him save Himself!" Many laughed and made fun of Jesus. They shouted ugly things about Him. Even one of the criminals joined in. "Save Yourself and us while You're at it!" But the other criminal scolded Him saying, "We deserve what we're getting, but this man has done nothing wrong."

"Father," Jesus prayed, "forgive all of these people. They do not know what they are doing." Then a deep darkness came over the land and the sun stopped shining. Jesus said, "Father, I give My life to You!" And He died.

At that moment, the curtain of the Temple tore from top to bottom. The earth shook and the rocks split. Tombs broke open and many dead people who had loved God during their lives were raised to life. They went into the city and many people saw them. Some of the soldiers who saw all of this were terrified and said, "Surely this was the Son of God!"

Jesus Is Alive!

Mark 16

After Jesus died, they put Him in a tomb and rolled a huge stone in front of it.

On the third day, women who loved Jesus went to the tomb. An angel of the Lord had rolled the stone away and was sitting on it. He was as bright as lightning and his robes were as white as snow.

"Do not be afraid," he said. "Jesus is alive again just like He said He would be." The women raced to tell the others, but they did not believe them.

That evening, Jesus appeared to all of His followers as they were hiding in a room having dinner. "Peace be with you!" Jesus said. They were so happy to see Him.

Thomas, who was not there, said, "I will not believe it until I see the nail marks and touch them with my fingers." A week later, Jesus appeared to them again. "Put your finger in My wounds, Thomas," Jesus said. "Stop doubting and believe." And Thomas did.

Jesus did many other amazing things – many of which were not written down. But these things are so you may believe that Jesus is the Son of God, and that by believing you may have life in Him.

For God loved the world so much that He gave His only Son so that anyone who believes in Him would live with Him forever.

Jesus gave one last command: "Tell everyone everywhere about Me. Whoever believes and is baptized will be saved, but whoever does not believe will be condemned."

While they watched, Jesus was taken high up into the sky until a cloud hid Him. As they squinted to see Him, two men in white robes suddenly stood near them. "Why are you still staring into the sky?" they asked. "Jesus has gone to heaven. And He will come back this very same way one day."

Amen, Lord. Come soon.